Building Bridges to the New Age World

LEARNING TO COMMUNICATE THE GOSPEL TO MODERN SPIRITUAL SEEKERS

Charles Strohmer

C O N T E N T S

CPAS © 1996

1

INTRODUCTION

As we head into the twenty-first century, one of the greatest challenges facing the Church is to learn how to communicate Christianly to what I sometimes call the fastest growing 'people group' in the world: New Age seekers. These modern spiritual seekers are into just about everything under the sun except those things that have to do with the Son.

Defining New Age thinking is no mean feat, and it is not the point of this book. But to say, as some do, that the New Age phenomenon is so fragmented and diverse that it's impossible to pin down some ultimate beliefs, is rather naive. Although New Age thinking is not formally recognized or strictly identifiable, a kind of DIY core is discernible (many followers, however, may not recognize what that core comprises). The more clearly identifiable of these underlying beliefs will come up for discussion throughout the following chapters.

The task before us here is to learn how to communicate effectively to these spiritual seekers. They are usually call New Agers and an avalanche of books since the 1980s has helped us to understand what they believe. But precious little has been produced (try to find it) to help us with the ins and outs of speaking to New Age people.

Our need in this area is great. Christians who sally forth to talk to New Age people often discover that it is like trying to make sense of a tornado! Ideas and beliefs scatter to the wind and seem to end up all over the map. What may have been a friendly, developing relationship becomes unsettled. Conversations escalate into little 'word wars' that result in offended feelings and alienation.

There must be a better way of listening to – and then communicating with – friends, colleagues and family members who are influenced by New Age thinking. It's a challenging task. This book aims to help ordinary Christians get to grips with it.

> **"Anyone who hopes to understand and cope with the contemporary western world needs to have some understanding of the New Age movement."**
>
> Lesslie Newbigin in Lawrence Osborn's *Angels of Light?*, Daybreak

---

Using this book

This is a practical book. Some will want to read it by themselves. However, the Group Focus activities at the end of each chapter make it an invaluable study for small groups. It is not a structured course, but the six chapters will help any group of people eager to move forward in communicating God's love and truth to today's spiritual seekers.

The author

Charles Strohmer is a writer, seminar speaker and ordained Christian minister. Based in Tennessee, USA, he travels widely and is the author of *What Your Horoscope Doesn't Tell You* and *Wise as a Serpent, Harmless as a Dove – Understanding and Communication in the New Age World* (Nelson Word Books), titled in the USA *The Gospel and the New Spirituality – Communicating the Truth in a World of Spiritual Seekers*, and *Explaining the Grace of God* (Sovereign World).

'... like trying to make sense of a tornado...'

AFTER AQUARIUS

New Age seekers are people with a highly experience-oriented spirituality. But they have no outside reference point (such as the Bible) to determine the validity of an experience. Just having an inner, mystical experience is what counts. Experience is trustworthy because 'it happened to me'. From the inner realm of self arises what is right and true. Experience is superior to truth.

Christians, too, believe in experience: our faith is not a dry, academic 'head knowledge'. But there is a difference. We believe we sense God's forgiveness because God actually has forgiven us – and the Bible tells us so. And even when we don't *feel* forgiven, we remind ourselves that 2000 years ago Christ died on the cross. Our experience is not just based on an encounter with God, but is backed up by history and the revelation of God in the Bible.

Today's spiritual seekers need no reference point like the Bible: their starting point for what they believe is solely their own experience. If they didn't experience it as true, then it isn't.

So the task of communication is great. Unfortunately, a disturbing trend is arising. Some church leaders are saying publicly that the New Age is passé. This is troubling not only because it is not true, but because it will throw Christians off the scent. We will be lulled into becoming passive where we ought to be active.

Out of Aquarius

When I became a Christian in 1976, after almost eight years as a New Ager, I needed a lot of help from the Church to get myself sorted out and to learn how to reach out to old friends who were still in the New Age world. Yet none of the various ministers or priests I talked to was of much help.

> **"In our time a step is being taken into a spiritual worldview. Let me stress that this is no dogma for which belief is demanded."**
>
> New Age thinker Sir George Trevelyan in Eddie and Debbie Shapiro's *The Way Ahead,* Element

'The Age of Aquarius?' they said; 'that went out with the Sixties. Not many people are into that anymore.'

'Are you sure?' I would say. 'Its beliefs are being caught by more and more people. Its leading thinkers are trying to spread these ideas throughout culture just like we Christians are trying to do with our views. If it *seems* like it has disappeared, that's because it's not in the media now, and because the ideas are becoming more sophisticated, less identifiable.'

'We'll have to wait and see what happens, Charles. In the meantime....' And so it went on.

'That went out with the Sixties...'

CHAPTER ONE

The paradigm shift

Changing 'the big picture' Christians did not seem to understand the huge change of the culture's beliefs, values, assumptions and attitudes – the 'paradigm shift' – that was taking place around them. A 'paradigm' is a large body of thought that is used to explain certain phenomena. A 'paradigm shift' occurs when a reigning paradigm can no longer explain new evidence that has accumulated. When the process reaches a certain pitch, a new structure of thought must arise to make sense of the new situation.

The most famous example of a paradigm shift happened some 400 years ago. People stopped believing that the sun travelled around the earth; they recognized that the earth is part of a solar system, and travels around the sun.

Age of Reason? It was a leap forward in knowledge that had a profound effect in the West on our understanding of ourselves and of our place in the universe. It helped to pave the way for the so-called Age of Reason (or 'Enlightenment') of the eighteenth century when much of our modern way of thinking emerged, especially our belief in the supremacy of human reason and our faith in scientific progress.

> **"Within the world-view of modern western culture...[t]he whole method of inquiry and discussion simply excludes the possibility that it might actually be the case that the one who created and sustains the entire universe of created beings has made himself known at a certain time and place in universal history."**
>
> Lesslie Newbigin, *Foolishness to the Greeks,* SPCK

This led to the assumption that God and religion are matters of private opinion, because we have taken it for granted that there is an irreconcilable difference between matters of faith and matters of fact. Society as we know it today, or 'modernism', as it is often called, was born.

Modernism The organizing principle of modernism can be summed up with the words: all that is seen can explain all that is. That is, the modern age was increasingly drawn away from any sort of spiritual orientation in the 'bread and butter' of life. Spirituality was for religion, while politics, business, science, medicine, family life (for many people), and even education (at least in the States) were slowly absorbed into a human-centred paradigm. It became unthinkable, as least for those professing themselves wise, to include acknowledgement of God in their view of the world.

Furthermore, this way of thinking, with its emphasis on scientific analysis, separated life into an almost infinite number of unrelated pieces. As knowledge became more and more specialized, it became increasingly difficult to grasp it all. Hence the rise of the 'specialist'. Life was no longer a whole; it was fragments and disconnections, and a universe of specialists was needed to analyze them.

There must be more During the mid-to-late twentieth century, people have become increasingly dissatisfied with this modernist paradigm. We have become painfully aware of the darker consequences of our reliance on human reason and scientific progress alone.

In so many words, many thoughtful people now admit publicly *that all that is seen is not explaining all that is.* 'There must be more to life than meets the eye,' they say. The established paradigm is no longer plausible. Hence, the openness of so many people to 'alternative' religions and spiritualities, particularly those with an eastern, 'holistic' emphasis.

> **"The New Age dawned in our generation in the West – in California – and moved east to Europe and Asia. The established order was reversed. The material universe ceased to be the ultimate reality, people began to seek the spiritual, mystical, occult, extra-terrestrial reality. Faith in 'intuition' or 'revelation' channelled by spirit entities, replaced the earlier 'modern' faith in human reason."**
>
> Vishal Mangalwadi, *In Search of Self: Beyond the New Age*, Spire

Recent history

This spiritual pioneering began by fits and starts with the 'Beats' of the 1950s. From the experiences they derived from Buddhism and hashish, people like Alan Watts, Jack Kerouac and Allen Ginsberg threw down the gauntlet and challenged the established paradigm. In answer to the question, 'What are you rebelling against?', Ginsberg read his poem 'Howl' to a San Francisco audience in 1955. It railed against a society whose 'mind is pure machinery, whose love is endless oil and stone, whose soul is electricity and banks.' Powerful stuff.

Then came the 1960s counter-culture. An increasing number of people, who would not consider themselves Christians, began to see the need for a new cultural paradigm for a new age, one that looked at life as a whole, with spirituality informing that whole. Many people looked to the stars for it – the 'Age of Aquarius' – to dawn. This would end the so-called 'Christian era' and usher in 2000 years of great transcendence and spirituality. Not a few 'Aquarians'

had a sharp native intelligence. By the late 1970s and throughout the 1980s, they had become influential leaders and well known for developing spiritual ways to raise their families and to do art, music, science, business, medicine, politics and education.

When I was a new Christian in the mid-1970s, most Christians could not seem to get their minds around this. All they had noticed was the disappearance of the long-haired hippies. No more Woodstocks or Beatles or marijuana or student protests. When people like myself tried to explain that we were not dealing merely with behavioural patterns or a few statements of belief, but something much deeper, we were usually dismissed by church leaders as being overly zealous or even misguided.

Leaving the underground

The Aquarians had not disappeared. They just did not look and sound the same. In the 1970s, outside the media spotlight, the Aquarians were finding ways around their off-putting terminology. It was a language barrier that prevented many westerners from coming on board because the ideas and concepts were too occult-sounding to people still influenced by a Jewish / Christian ethos.

Thus the 1980s became rife with so-called New Age ideas, beliefs and practices largely because the language barrier was bypassed by using inoffensive terms and euphemisms. For example:

- ○ The 'Age of Aquarius' became the 'New Age';
- ○ Psychic healing techniques became 'therapeutic touch';
- ○ Hatha yoga was often known as 'stress relaxation management';
- ○ Forms of occult meditation became 'centring', 'stilling', 'grounding', 'going within';
- ○ Witchcraft was called 'wicca';
- ○ Spirit mediums became 'channellers' and their spirits, 'channelled energies' or 'spirit guides'.

5

> **"One of the biggest advantages we have as New Agers is, once the occult, metaphysical and New Age terminology is removed, we have concepts and techniques that are very acceptable to the general public. So we change the names and demonstrate the power. In so doing, we open the door to millions who normally would not be receptive."**
>
> Dick Sutphen, New Age activist, writing in the 1980s

Early Christian response

In the 1980s Christian analyses of every sort broke out about the 'New Age Movement'. Books and seminars were helpful among ourselves, but little, if anything, was being produced about the paradigm shift or to help us solve the riddle of communicating with New Age people. We could deconstruct the New Age worldview, but we could not construct a communication bridge to the people in that world.

Today, on the cusp of a new century, when energetic discussion about communicating to the New Age 'people group' ought to be taking place in our churches and mission conferences, we are falling prey to the same kind of naiveté as we did in the 1970s: the New Age is being considered passé. It is tempting to think this because, as in the 1970s, the media are not mentioning it as much, and because the current emphasis on church renewal and 'spiritual warfare' is so strong.

This is a huge mistake. Indeed, although masses of people still remain aloof to New Age spirituality, the phenomenon is expanding, not contracting. Followers are being added regularly – at a rate which at times rivals any church growth programmes!

Just as mature Christians bring their worldview to bear upon the spheres of culture in which they find themselves (workplace, family, recreation), so do New Age people, who are becoming more and more adept at influencing culture. As a result, Christians who live, work and play alongside modern spiritual seekers find that it is very difficult to know what to say to them. Christians who have tried will tell you how exasperating the experience can be.

Reaching out

So we are not dealing with a fad or a conspiracy or a lunatic fringe of environmentalists. We are dealing with a paradigm shift, one that is as profound as the cultural transitions from the Renaissance into the Reformation and from the Reformation into the Enlightenment period. And in this new paradigm, many people are bringing an eastern holistic spirituality to bear upon modern life.

Lawrence Osborn has written, 'The New Age movement represents millions of spiritual aspirants who are sickened by the cruder materialism of culture.' And, might I add, by a Church so often caught up in modernism that it does not know how to offer spiritual seekers the one true Alternative?

Churches, parachurch organizations and missions groups everywhere are currently equipping Christians to 'evangelize the world for Christ'. Let's include the New Age people group. Let's not get caught short again, just because the media emphases are elsewhere, or because other matters also need attention.

One thing we know so far: it is not enough merely to know what non-Christian spiritual seekers believe. Although this has not been our strong suit to date, this alone has not been able to make us effective communicators in the New Age world. This is because New Age people have particular intellectual and spiritual dynamics that seriously frustrate Christian communication. We need to learn how to get around these dynamics in order to have effective communication.

New Age Worldview

AIM **To provide an introduction to some basic New Age assumptions.**

It is tempting not to include this page. It tends to over-simplify New Age views, as if it were possible to say, 'We've read the list. Now we understand.' Nevertheless a core of New Age ideas is identifiable and it may be helpful to have a list of them. Many of these topics are expanded in Chapter 4, in the context of the communication problems they pose.

- God is an impersonal cosmic energy, or force.
- The universe is that cosmic energy in a highly concentrated form: energy 'congealed' as matter. It includes both inanimate and animate life, including human beings.
- God and the universe – all inanimate and animate life, the seen and the unseen – are one and divine.
- No ultimate, or fundamental, distinctions exist between God, inanimate reality and animate life. The rock, the star, the tree, the beetle, the whale, the human being – indeed, everything – ultimately makes up an undifferentiated divine whole.
- Life is also morally one; there are no absolute moral distinctions between good and evil; all religions are one.
- Human nature has no limits. Even death is merely a door to spiritual evolution.
- The human problem is its 'limited awareness' or 'narrow consciousness'; human beings view life in pieces instead of as a whole. The solution is 'consciousness expansion'.
- The human problem is basically one of 'bad karma' – the combined results of our bad actions in previous existences. 'Salvation' is through reincarnation; birth and death are merely stages in one vast 'spiritual evolution'.

- The human problem is also connected to our forgetfulness, or ignorance, of our divine nature and oneness with all things. 'Salvation' is enlightenment or self-realization – a reawakening to our divinity and oneness with all things.
- Reason and belief (often called 'left-brain' thinking) are barriers to enlightenment, and the solution is to jump into the irrational and trust 'intuition'. 'Truth' is solely within and is relative.
- Consciousness-expansion techniques (often called 'right-brain' creativity) are used to perceive, control and then reverse the effects of the human problem; these may produce an alleged 'mystical' experience of oneness with the divine.
- History is cyclical.
- Jesus Christ is one of many 'avatars' – one of the manifestations of the divine in human form (like Buddha or Krishna) who appears every so often with a powerful message for humankind.
- The supernatural world comprises helpful 'spirit guides' which may be contacted through 'channelling'. They are supposedly former human beings who have 'paid off' all their bad karma, and so no longer need to be reincarnated, but are now spirit entities. If humans are highly evolved at death, they can become 'spirit guides'.

This looks complicated – a set of beliefs that you'd only find in one person in a million. But most of us have at least one friend who believes that God isn't a person, but 'some sort of force', or one or two other friends who feel they 'need to get in touch with themselves' and maybe some workmates who are interested in aromatherapy, horoscopes and reincarnation. These people may not be wearing a New Age seeker's life-jacket, but they are paddling in the New Age pool of beliefs and values. They are not far from the underlying New Age assumption that 'All is One; One is All; All is God'.

The New Age in the World and in My Backyard

1. MEDIA WATCH
To help participants discern New Age thinking.

Invite group members to bring New Age magazines, books or newspaper and magazine articles about the New Age, or New Age brochures and advertisements. Leaving aside the more obvious New Age beliefs and practices, such as astrology or crystal therapy, ask people to describe why they think an article, idea or practice is 'New Age'.

People's comments may include:

references to cosmic energies   *profiles of New Age gurus or thinkers*
comments in letters to the editor   *advertisements for body, mind, spirit festivals*
emphases on intuitive, inner experiences   *mention of reincarnation*
reference to business training methods seeking to 'maximize human potential'

Christians often have a hunch that something is 'New Age', without being able to give a specific reason for that feeling. There's nothing wrong with such uncertainty. What matters is being willing to try to articulate your hunches, and don't worry if they sound silly. The best insights often begin at that point! (Use the 'New Age Worldview Checklist' to prime the pump.)

2. ON OUR DOORSTEP
To help group members appreciate that New Age influences are closer to us than we might imagine.

Some Christians still think that the New Age is 'out there somewhere'. It's someone else's problem. But that is rarely the case. Usually it is a mistake to think that it's not a local phenomenon. Invite people to say where they have seen New Age influences in their neighbourhood, town or locality – perhaps even in their own family. You may be surprised to see how prevalent it is in your own backyard.

Examples could be taken from:

newspaper stories   *school events*   *local events*   *health care providers*
television /radio programmes   *neighbours*   *advertisements for psychic fairs or mediums*

Use your discussion to compile a list of near-at-hand New Age activities. Keep the list, possibly arranging for every member of the group to have a copy. By the end of these sessions, you should feel more confident about talking to the people involved in such activities, and to people who are influenced by them. As you work through this book, make mental or written notes of any ideas that strike you as appropriate ways of approaching and speaking to these people. Later, try out these ideas. Don't be afraid to fail – making mistakes can be a great teacher. More likely, you'll be pleasantly surprised at your successes.

For prayer Ask God for sensitivity and discernment as you think of possible contacts with New Age people.

MODELS OR MUDDLES?

'Everyone speaks well of the bridge that carries him over,' says an ancient proverb.

New Age enthusiasts may speak favourably of a Christian message when we have built suitable communication bridges into their lives.

"I could see how difficult it is to evangelize pantheists who believe that they are already divine, have endless potential for self-improvement, are not inherently sinful, and not in need of the gracious once-for-all provision of Jesus Christ's atonement."

Gordon R Lewis in Douglas Groothuis' *Unmasking the New Age,* IVP

Communication bridges

Building communication bridges is not about:

○ reciting the right texts
○ applying formulas
○ using methods
○ learning a bag of tricks
○ engaging in a contest of wills

These and other ploys like treating people as evangelization 'projects' put unnecessary strain on conversation, give rise to hostile feelings and alienate us from the very people we are called to help.

Communication bridges are built as a result of forming relationships with people. Some Christians find this difficult in the New Age world, usually because of unnecessary and unhealthy fears. Nevertheless, communication, by its very nature, takes place between people. And relationships of some sort must be established in order for effective communication to occur.

Submarines and warships

One thing we need to learn is how to stop sinking submarines! In my book *Wise as a Serpent, Harmless as a Dove,* I have developed at length what I call the 'submarine model' of communication. Here is the idea in brief.

Most of us have seen those old World War Two movies in which allied warships spot an enemy submarine floating on the surface of the ocean. What happens on board the sub when this occurs? Panic strikes. Klaxon horns blare ominously, submariners scurry to their posts, the clamour inside the sub becomes interminable and over the intercom the voice of command cries, 'Dive! Dive!' Meanwhile, the battleships are blasting away with their big guns from a great distance hoping to shoot holes in the submarine before it submerges.

Figuratively speaking, not a few modern spiritual seekers react like this whenever they see Christians approaching. Christians look like enemy warships

CPAS © 1996

'Dive! Dive! Christian approaching!'

> **"One of the greatest hindrances to the communication of the Christian message to those of [another] worldview has been the communicator himself."**
>
> David Burnett, *Clash of Worlds*, Nelson

with guns a-blazing and New Age people cannot react fast enough to get out of the way. Their radar sounds: 'Dive! Dive! Get out of the way. Christian approaching!'

It is not uncommon for a Christian to lose the New Age person below the surface of communication. You are talking to her and suddenly the horizon is empty. She has not physically disappeared: rather, you have lost contact with her intellectually. She had been buoyant, listening, floating nicely on the surface of communication, but then you said or did something, probably unwittingly, that sent the wrong signal to the sub's radar. You are seen as a threat and she dives below the surface of communication. She is no longer really engaged in the conversation with you, no longer listening. She may eventually wind up leagues away from what you are saying if you don't work to correct the situation – that is, refloat the submarine by restoring conversational equilibrium.

Transforming our appearance

One way to start correcting this situation is to change the way we look. How about this: instead of appearing as threatening battleships, what if we appeared more like luxury cruise liners? We might look more appealing. Perhaps, then, non-Christian spiritual seekers would let us float alongside them. Perhaps they would even ask us where we are headed.

Eventually they might even ask how they could get on board with us. After all, isn't that the goal?

Coming alongside New Age people in an appealing way is not easy for some Christians: they assume that it means making ungodly compromises. But the Submarine Communications Model is not about giving up biblical truth or capitulating to false beliefs or forbidden practices. It is about 'principled conversation', what I often call the 'sensitive but firm approach', and it makes possible healthy relationships and effective communication with New Age seekers. This will help to keep the subs floating, keep spiritual seekers listening.

'...if we appeared more like cruise liners?'

Four levels of spiritual seeking

Another way to keep New Age people floating on the surface of communication is to be sensitive to the different kinds of people you will meet. People have varying degrees of interest in so-called New Age ideas and practices, and this may make a difference in how we approach and talk with them. I keep four broad categories in mind, although there is much ebb and flow among them.

The border people

This large group is found on the fringes of the New Age world. They only have superficial or casual spiritual interests, which may not deepen at all but may, for whatever reasons, eventually pass. These folk probably do not even have a conscious sense that they are flirting with 'New Age' attitudes.

The seekers

This group is more consciously influenced by New Age ideas and practices. We will find many such people. They are aware of the New Age world, and they have seen and heard enough to make a decision to dive in at some level. They have probably read a book or two on New Age themes, and they may be getting involved in New Age practices. They are 'seeking'.

The enthusiasts

This group lies farther along the continuum, and in a sense the people in this group are not really seekers. That is, they have not stopped their spiritual journey; they would not say that they have 'arrived'. But they have experienced enough to decide that they will carry out their spiritual sojourn only within a New Age worldview. They usually have a good deal of their lives organized around New Age living, and they can 'give a reason' for what they believe. They are advanced 'seekers'.

The spokespersons

A final distinction that I have found helpful in my line of work is the 'spokesperson'. The people in this group often manage or own New Age shops or clinics. They may be therapists, seminar speakers or authors. They are the professionals.

> **"Each age offers its own particular challenge to Christianity. Because unbelief can take many forms, those learning 'to give a reason for the hope that [they] have' (1 Peter 3:15) need to be sensitive to the audience they are addressing yet not so 'sensitive' that the Gospel is altered to suit modern tastes."**
>
> Douglas Groothuis, *Confronting the New Age*, IVP

Approaching the various levels

When approaching modern spiritual seekers, I have found it very beneficial to try immediately to determine where along the continuum the person falls. This can prevent a lot of headaches up front, and it can keep us from causing unnecessary offence. Here are a few short illustrations to get you thinking in this vein.

Speaking to a *border person* as if she were an *enthusiast* will quickly drive the person below the surface of communication. She will see you as being heavy-handed and wonder what all the fuss is about. For example, she may mention 'reincarnation' because it's just a term she heard in passing. She may have no more interest in it than you do. On the other hand, if you speak to *enthusiasts* or *spokespersons* as if the New Age were merely nonsense, you will never have their ear either.

Since *seekers* are still undecided about many New Age things, they will be open to Christian discussion of issues that *enthusiasts* and *spokespersons* may not be. For instance, *seekers* will usually listen to an opposing point of view, sensitively put. They may even be open to an invitation from you to visit the activities that go on around your church.

CPAS © 1996

11

Try to discover if *border people* or *seekers* have what we might call a residual Christian memory, perhaps from their family upbringing or from attending church during their youth. This memory may still carry some clout with the person when it is appealed to. A contrast between basic biblical doctrines, such as creation, the fall, sin and redemption, and New Age views can be quite influential with such people.

Enthusiasts or *spokespersons,* however, are usually turned off by anything to do with Christianity. This means that we will have to find a different starting point, or common ground elsewhere. One approach that may be necessary with *enthusiasts* or *spokespersons* is to be alert to any hurts or wounds that may have been caused by Christians. Until we learn how to apply balm to these wounds, we will not get much of a hearing.

A risk and a breakthrough

The force of this came ringing home to me during a radio debate with a New Age author who was also a medium. During the debate the medium became extremely defensive toward me, which surprised even the presenter because I had not given her any reason to be angry at me. In fact, knowing that she was a *spokesperson,* I tried my best not to upset her.

About halfway through the debate, I suspected that she had been offended by Christians, and that she was taking those deep frustrations out on me. So right there on that radio programme I took a risk and broached the subject with her. She told us about the way some Christians had been treating her, and it was easy to appreciate why she was upset with the lot of us. I knew then what I had to do.

As an official representative of the Christian faith (being an ordained minister), I earnestly apologized to her for the terrible way in which she had been treated. 'I don't believe it!' she blurted out, pleasantly surprised. 'A Christian who understands. Thank you for what you just said. I never thought I'd hear that.'

This defused the entire situation. The woman's

expression changed, and so did the entire atmosphere in that radio studio. We were able to conduct the last half of that debate without that ugly tension in the air, or on the air! This woman was so affected by my 'apology' that after the radio programme she invited me to spend some more time talking with her. Here was a person who was solidly floating on the surface of communication.

Towards a new view

Another way to make a beginning at effective communication is to have the best possible understanding of the New Age phenomenon. Numerous models have been tried over the years. Unhelpful models are:

- ○ the fad model
- ○ the conspiracy model
- ○ the demon-monger model
- ○ the movement model

Trying to understand New Age thinking as a 'movement' was by far the best of these four models. But I no longer believe that it is suitable, for it does not carry within it all that we now know about the social-spiritual phenomenon called 'New Age'.

Some analysts call it a 'new paradigm', and others a 'worldview'. Fair enough. But there has been so much emphasis on paradigms and worldviews during the past twenty years that both are now subtly taken to mean only a set of ideas, a mindset. That is, they tend to divorce ideas, values, beliefs and assumptions from daily, practical living.

Two wisdoms

We know that the Bible does not disassociate our ideas, beliefs and values from our actions and behaviour. Searching for a model that includes both areas, I have found St Paul's teaching on wisdom in 1 Corinthians 1 and 2 to be invaluable. It has had the additional benefit of surprising me with considerable help for solving the kinds of communication riddles we face with spiritual seekers.

> **"For the message of the cross is foolishness to those who are perishing, but to us who are being saved it is the power of God.... We do, however, speak a message of wisdom among the mature, but not the wisdom of this age or of the rulers of this age, who are coming to nothing. No, we speak of God's secret wisdom...."**
>
> 1 Corinthians 1:18; 2:6-7

In these two well-known chapters St Paul is contrasting two wisdoms: that of the world, or humankind, with God's wisdom expressed in Jesus Christ.

But what does St Paul mean by 'wisdom'? In *Wisdom in the Marketplace*, theologian John Peck tells us that in the Bible 'wisdom' is about both theory and practice. That is, wisdom is a way of seeing life and behaving in accordance with how you see it.

Wisdom, therefore, is not merely head knowledge. According to the Bible it links ideas, values and beliefs with our actions and behaviour. It is a way of seeing life and behaving in it. It is a way of making sense of creation and living it. A simple axiom may be: wisdom is applied knowledge (applied both consciously and subconsciously).

In short, wisdom relates theory to practice. St Paul is therefore saying that non-Christians make sense of the creation and live in it according to the sense *they* make of it, and that Christians see life and behave in it according to the sense *they* make of it. And both do this in a very a different way.

For example, Tom 'sees' life as fundamentally an impersonal cosmic energy or force (a kind of spiritual electricity) of which human beings are made – that is his underlying belief. Particular actions and behaviour will flow from that belief: Tom will want to practise techniques for 'tapping into' that energy. These may include forms of meditation, advanced yoga techniques or making contact with spirit guides.

Conversely, Jane's underlying belief is that behind all life there is a personal infinite creator God. Her outer practices – among them prayer and praise – reflect that inner belief in a God with whom we may have a relationship.

Paul is quick to recognize that attempts to communicate between the two different wisdoms may cause severe headaches. This is implied in his statements about the 'foolishness' that appears to exist between them (1 Corinthians 1:18, 20, 25). It is possible for one wisdom to look at the ideas, beliefs and lifestyle of the other wisdom and ridicule them. And the other may return the favour!

13

CHAPTER TWO

The wisdom model

Perhaps you can see what I'm leading up to: the use of the 'wisdom model' for understanding the New Age phenomenon and for communicating to its adherents. New Age people, like everyone else, have a way of making sense of the world in order to live in it effectively; they have a way of seeing life that influences their actions. That is to say, they have a certain 'wisdom' for life. And the trick is to learn how to communicate our 'foolishness' (1 Corinthians 1:21) to theirs!

different. New Age seekers may barely understand our questions, comments and ideas, and we may barely understand theirs, even though we are both speaking the same language – English. This poses great communication riddles. 'Foolishness' is the name of bridge that must be crossed between the two wisdoms in order for effective communication to begin.

Tom Why do you Christians pray? There's no need for that. We are all part of God. You just need to tap into your Higher Self.

Jane Why do you New Agers refuse to believe in God? You need to ask God to forgive you.

Tom No. My problem is my bad karma from my past lives. I just need to pay that off with my good deeds.

Jane No. You're a sinner. You need to accept Jesus into your life.

And on and on it goes. There's no real communication here. Tom and Jane are merely becoming increasingly entrenched in their respective positions.

Throughout this book you will hear me talk about New Age wisdom. Between New Age wisdom and Christian wisdom lies a great intellectual and spiritual gulf that must be bridged in order for effective communication to occur.

In the two wisdoms, the basic assumptions about God, humanity, the universe, the future and so on are

> **"Wisdom [in the Bible] is a word about the sort of sense you make of creation in order to live in it effectively (it will affect what you think is effective living, too)."**
>
> John Peck, *Wisdom in the Marketplace*, Greenbelt Festivals

Meeting Success and Failure

1. A QUESTION OF FEELINGS

To explain some of the feelings, difficulties and successes participants have had when talking to New Age people.

Normally confident Christians can find it unusually difficult to communicate effectively to New Age people. Invite group members to describe how they feel when approaching a spiritual seeker:

calm   nervous   delighted   upset
wishing you were somewhere else   other:

Invite group members to recall a time when they may have 'sunk a submarine'. Perhaps it was as a result of:

anger   arguing   trying to save face   badgering   other:

Others, however, have had some successes. No 'success' is a minor success in this important field!

Ask members of the group to describe a way in which they have built an effective communication bridge to a spiritual seeker. It may be something quite simple. Alternatively, ask people to describe how they think we should start the process. For example:

• *in a short-term context (for example, a conversation on a bus)*
• *in a long-term relationship (for example, a neighbour or a person at work)*

2. WHAT'S IT ALL ABOUT?
To help participants see how views of the New Age have changed over the years.

Ask group members to describe the variety of ways in which it's possible to describe the New Age phenomenon:

bad   conspiracy   entirely occult   a good thing
a worldview   part of a wider 'human potential movement'   other:

Do any members of the group identify with any of the above views?
Invite people to explain their views.
Ask if anyone has experienced a change of view? How did such a change come about?

> **For prayer** Focus on the importance of being good listeners.

CPAS © 1996

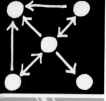

Same Diagnosis, Different Prescription?

 AIM To see that the New Age is an understandable but non-Christian response to modernism; to appreciate that Christianity offers a far more radical response to modernism than does the New Age.

Introduction

The New Age is in part a reaction to disillusionment with the long-standing western paradigm (way of thinking) that often goes by the name of modernism.

Humanity, not God, is at the heart of modernism. It is based on the belief that men and women alone are responsible for themselves and for their planet's future. Modernism idolizes human reason, the individual, industry, science, technology and economics. These, of course, are all valid in themselves. Our problems begin when we elevate them into idols. It is then that injustice and other problems slowly become apparent.

The second half of our century has seen increasing numbers of people reacting against modernism, exploring what they see as its opposites. Many people have therefore moved towards 'alternative' spiritualities, in which intuition is set against the rational, mysticism against materialism. Others have reacted against individualism by searching for new forms of community.

It is important to understand that New Age thinking is a reaction to modernism and not, in the first place, to Christianity. Although it is unlikely that we will accept the solutions that New Age thinking offers to modernism, we may be able to agree with some of the New Age analyses of its problems.

Christianity offers a profound alternative both to modernism's way of making sense of the world (a paradigm that is nearing its sell-by date) and to the New Age's response to it.

What to do

Make enough copies of the chart on the facing page to give to each member of the group. The left-hand column has been filled in with some fundamental points of modernism. As a group, fill in the middle column by referring to the 'Worldview Checklist' at the end of Chapter 1. Fill in the right-hand column from what you know about Christianity as you discuss these points around the group.

Finally

Please keep in mind that, like the 'Worldview Checklist' in Chapter 1, this activity cannot give you a thorough understanding of the New Age or an accurate picture of a New Age person. This is because people are complex. They hold to values and beliefs from many different, and at times, conflicting views. And they usually do this unknowingly. For example, many Christians will hold to some values of modernism. Modernists will hold to some Christian values, and New Agers will still be working out of some modernist, or even some Christian, ideas.

For prayer Ask God for a renewed sense of wonder at the radically good news of the gospel of Jesus Christ.

MODERNISM (or 'traditional secular attitudes')	NEW AGE	CHRISTIANITY
God is • non-existent or • very far away and irrelevant to public life	**God is**	**God is**
Jesus is • merely a good man, • if he ever existed at all	**Jesus is**	**Jesus is**
Creation is • not created, • but self-existent, • evolving	**Creation is**	**Creation is**
Human beings are • merely atoms / brains / animals • the centre of all things • merely members of society • inherently good	**Human beings are**	**Human beings are**
Salvation is • unnecessary • rationality and control • achievable through science, technology and economics	**Salvation is**	**Salvation is**
Life after death is • non-existent • unknown and uncertain • not worth thinking about	**Life after death is**	**Life after death is**

IN THE NEW AGE WORLD

It is easy to say that we must be clear and understandable in our communications. Recognizing that doing so can take some effort is another matter.

There is the story of the concerned mother who came upon her dejected five-year-old late one afternoon:

'What's wrong, David? How come you're not outside playing?'
'My teacher called me names today,' little David replied sulkily.
'Oh, I don't think Mrs Green would do that, do you? She's a nice lady.'
'Yes, she did. She called me a scurvy elephant.'
'Well, you're certainly not a scurvy elephant, are you? Now run along and play.'

This calls for a chat with Mrs Green, thought David's mother. I'll see if I can speak to her when I drop David off at school tomorrow morning.

'Scurvy elephant? No, no,' said Mrs Green. 'David was getting a little out of hand yesterday, and I asked him not to be such a disturbing element.'

Nothing for granted
Unfortunately, all too often this could be an apt illustration of what communication between Christians and non-Christian spiritual seekers is like.

> **"Christians should remember that sensitivity to the leading of the Holy Spirit is crucial for any apologetic or evangelistic encounter so that, in Paul's words, 'our faith might not rest on men's wisdom, but on God's power' (1 Corinthians 2:5)."**
> Douglas Groothuis, *Confronting the New Age*, IVP

We can never take successful communication for granted. Even a married couple celebrating their fiftieth wedding anniversary may still have communication problems. So how much more care is needed in a conversation between two people who may not know each other very well, or who may even feel suspicious or hostile towards one another? That's when it is very easy to sink submarines.

Let's take a few minutes to look at several dynamics that may hinder the communication process – and at ways of getting around them.

> **"Familiarity breeds inattention."**
> G K Chesterton

Failing to relate to persons
Failing to relate to people as persons may be at the heart of all failed communication. We may get so caught up in the conversation, so proud of our position, so sure of ourselves, so intense and zealous, that we forget that a person is on the receiving end. We may treat people like mere objects, things, viewpoints, or, God forbid, entities from 'the other side'. In short, sometimes we are so used to talking to people that we forget what they are – persons.

Conversations and relationships, however, are with people. It is people that Jesus calls, and people that we are called to reach. Now people are complex, unpredictable, emotional. They have strong likes and dislikes. Thus they are prone to human reactions and need to be approached as individuals.

Though New Age people may have different backgrounds from ours, and though they may easily get frustrated, angry or offended with us, we still must work to get around these communication barriers. We can do this by creating trust, recognition and respect in the relationship.

- *Trust* If we want the person to trust in the Lord, are we making it difficult for him or her to first trust us? Why should the person trust Christ if he or she cannot trust Christ's messenger?

- *Recognition* A person's value and good points ought to be recognized. Not only are these people for whom Jesus died, but, sin aside, they have strengths, insights, and ways of living that are worth affirming.

- *Respect* Courtesy and appreciation go a long way. So does giving the other person the opportunity to talk, to explain a position, to be opinionated. When our mouths are on automatic pilot, we send a message that we think the other person has nothing important or relevant to say. That is a disrespectful attitude. Cultivating trust, recognition and respect is a powerful communication bridge-builder.

Identifying with a caricature

It is easy to draw mental images of people that prevent us from relating to them as persons. Caricatures are created by the labels we put on people. 'She's a New Ager'; 'He's an occultist'; 'What a ridiculous view!' Labels are depersonalizing. How beside the point it is when Christians point to a celebrity with New Age connections and say, 'Shirley MacLaine – that zany redhead with her crazy ideas. She's nuts!', or 'David Icke? He used to be so sensible.' Such ridicule is uncalled-for. And it's on our lips too often. It blinds us to the fact that people like MacLaine have a sharp native intelligence and are on a spiritual journey.

'New Age caricatures are depersonalizing...'

> **"Your neighbour, your child's teacher, or your friend may believe he's found the truth in the promises of the New Age. So how do you introduce him to Christ as Truth – and Saviour – when his belief system says there are many paths to God? New Agers must be approached as individuals, with sensitivity and real understanding that is stripped of stereotypes."**
>
> Dean Halverson, *Crystal Clear: Understanding and Reaching New Agers*, Navpress

Caricatures affect the expectations we have of people. Such expectations will probably evoke responses from us that are caricatures themselves.

Of course, spiritual seekers may return the favour and perceive us as caricatures! To them, we may be behind-the-times, narrow-minded, superstitious and a host of other discrediting adjectives.

Many people's attitude to Christians is based on a perception of a kind of vague 'background' Christianity in contemporary western culture. It is a distortion of the love, teaching and Saviour at the heart of authentic Christianity. It is a kind of rumour, reflected in the biased views that are presented in much of the media – and for many people, it is all they know about Christianity.

To amend Nathaniel's words when he was called by Philip to follow Jesus, '*Christianity! Can any good thing come from there?*' (John 1:46). If this is the case, we will have to work hard to dispel such images. For there is no such thing as caricature-to-caricature communication.

19

CHAPTER THREE

So our task in this area is twofold. We must discard our caricatures of others, and we must be sensitive to caricatures others may have of us.

Sounding like the demanding boss

If you want to get off to a bad start with spiritual seekers, this is the best way, as I have found out many times! The Christian who sounds like a demanding boss undermines the communication process. Here is the judge, the dogmatist, the professor looking down his nose from the podium, lecturing and creating distance from his audience. It took me a long time to stop sinking submarines like this!

'Sounding like the demanding boss....'

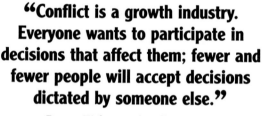

"Conflict is a growth industry. Everyone wants to participate in decisions that affect them; fewer and fewer people will accept decisions dictated by someone else."

Roger Fisher and William Ury,
Getting to Yes, Penguin

The demanding boss, or lecturing parent, is full of 'do nots', 'must nots' and 'ought nots'.

○ He lays down rules and laws.
○ He is hypercritical or negative toward those who don't share his beliefs.
○ He is often heard saying, 'Don't you know that's wrong? You shouldn't be doing that.'

When the spiritual seeker hears the demanding boss, he may be reminded of a strict parent who criticized, ridiculed or talked down to him when he was a child.

○ The spiritual seeker will never know that the Christian is someone with Good News when all he's hearing is so much bad news.
○ There is no grace seasoned with salt on the lips of the demanding boss.

Adult-to-adult conversation

The solution is to have adult-to-adult exchanges in which the submarine stays floating on the surface of communication.

Try to be conversational. Talk to seekers as you would talk to a prospective buyer of your house, or as you would talk to your spouse about where to go for dinner. This builds effective communication bridges.

Expressing inappropriate emotions

Emotions and feelings play a big role in the communication process. Both parties bring a mixture of them into a conversation, and these can help to float or sink submarines.

How do you feel toward spiritual seekers?

○ Some Christians exhibit an unhealthy fear. A suspicious or fearful Christian may trigger an equal and opposite reaction from the listener. Thinking he is under attack, the seeker will drop below the surface of communication.
○ Others Christians may be overly nervous, suspicious, upset, worried, even angry. As a result, seekers may become defensive and angry.
○ Christians who are relaxed and confident help spiritual seekers settle into conversations.

20

'Aim for adult to adult conversation.'

Some communication headaches, therefore, are not relieved from a better understanding of the person's viewpoint or ideas, but through better control over one's emotions and feelings.

○ If you have control over your tone of voice, you are probably in control of your emotions. Perhaps the best tone of voice is the one in which it is evident to the listener that you are teachable, for it sends the signal of a willingness to learn.

Emotions and feelings can speak louder than words at times. Should your emotions start to run high, find ways to defuse the situation. Be honest with the other person about your feelings. This can help to restore conversational equilibrium. Talking to the other person about your feelings is all right. It does no harm to say: 'You know, I get the feeling that we are misunderstanding each other. Do you feel this way?' Or 'I'm sorry for getting upset. I suppose I'm a bit nervous.' It will feel good to the person who hears you say this. It will calm the atmosphere. Verbal conflicts that seem irredeemable can be cleared up through the sharing of feelings.

> **"Everyone should be quick to listen, slow to speak."**
> James 1:19

> **"One who cannot listen long and patiently will presently be talking beside the point, albeit he is not conscious of it."**
> Dietrich Bonhoeffer, *Life Together,*
> Harper & Row

Ears that don't hear

Sometimes we're not really listening because we think we know precisely what the other person is going to say, where the conversation is headed, and so in our minds we're preparing our rebuttal. Instead of really listening, we can't wait to have our say. At best, this is disrespectful – at worst, it is a form of insult. Try to listen actively when the seeker is talking.

A wit remarked that since we have two ears but only one mouth, perhaps this is God's way of indicating that we should listen twice as much as we speak.

A good listener listens actively. She pays attention. She remembers what has been said. She remembers the person's name, whether he is single or married, what his spiritual interests are. How embarrassing to be arranging another meeting and have to ask, 'What did you say your name was?' Surely the person must wonder what else you were not listening to.

A good listener is a person who is discerning and learning. Even Christians who are well-versed in New Age thinking may find they prefer to do more listening than speaking during a first-time conversation with a New Ager.

Some New Age seekers have had such negative experiences with Christians that the best thing we can do is to offer the ministry of listening. And maybe we will have to listen long and hard before we earn the right to a hearing.

21

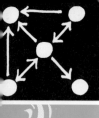

Attitude check

AIM **CHANGING OUR LOOKS**
To help participants avoid the 'stereotype barrier.'

When my wife Linda and I lived overseas on the mission field, we discovered that we had to dispel caricatures on two fronts: the first was how the nationals looked at us as Americans; the other was how they looked at us as Christians. Once we broke through these communication barriers – it took some work! – we were able to have meaningful conversations with our neighbours.

What kind of caricature do you think New Age people may have of you apart from your Christianity? What kind of a caricature do you think New Age people may have of you as a Christian?

superstitious   *behind-the-times*   *nationalistic, rationalistic, materialistic*
out of touch with reality   *uninformed*   *other:*

Choose areas group members have described and suggest ways of dispelling that caricature or stereotype. For example, if the seeker thought that you were 'out of touch with reality', a way ahead might be to express ways in which you are aware of current trends.

AIM **DID I SAY THAT?**
To help the group see the danger of 'demanding boss' exchanges.

Demanding boss exchange

Seeker I've had my horoscope done.
Christian Oh no! That's wrong. You're not supposed to get involved in the occult.

OR

Seeker I'm taking yoga classes.
Christian But that's not going to help you. Don't you know where that stuff comes from?

Adult-to-adult exchange

Christian What got you interested in astrology?
Seeker After my marriage broke up, a friend told me that my wife and I were not compatible. He introduced me to an astrologer who can tell me what kind of people I'm compatible with.
Christian I'm sorry that you got divorced. My sister went through a lot of pain when she divorced.
Seeker It was horrible. I don't want to make the same mistake again.
Christian Why do you think astrology can help?

Seeker I practise yoga – at quite an advanced level, actually.
Christian I know someone who tried yoga. She didn't get much out of it and stopped. How much time do you spend on it? Is it helping you?
Seeker I spend a couple of hours a week with it, but I don't know if it's helping me yet. But it's more than just exercises. There's a lot of meaning to the positions and some of them are pretty difficult to do.
Christian What got you interested?

For prayer Ask God to show us areas in which we might need to start 'changing our looks'.

ON COMMON GROUND

Here are several other ways to build effective communication bridges and to stop sinking submarines in New Age waters.

The question

Acquiring the knack of asking appropriate questions is a good way to keep spiritual seekers floating on the surface of communication. Questions help people to think, and so to stay engaged in the conversation. They also call for a response. Think of journalists with their microphones interviewing people. Their job is to inquire. And the answers they get are often quite revealing.

> **"Blasting away with straightforward statements usually generates more heat than light. Asking thoughtful questions often brings fresh insight."**

Tactful questions:
○ engage a person's attention
○ keep the conversation moving along
○ help the listener feel that he or she is on equal footing with the speaker
○ show that you are interested
○ help change subjects
○ free the speaker from sounding like the demanding boss or lecturing parent
○ help find a way through embarrassing situations
○ help with 'ownership' of difficult issues

When Job's 'counsellors' had exhausted all their formal theological statements in order to help him see the error of his ways, God deluged Job with questions. Questions can open people up to new, different and exciting, possibilities. Jesus used questions to lead seekers into the light, for questions can take a relationship deeper.

Signs of truth

When I am talking to a spiritual seeker, I look for what I call 'signs of truth' lurking around the person's wisdom. I try to direct the discussion toward them.

> **"The strength and subtlety of New Age largely lies in that it capitalizes on...areas which are fundamental to the...Christian message."**
>
> Jim Graham, *What Is The New Age?*, Hodder & Stoughton

New Age wisdom has an appeal because some of its beliefs, views and ideas deal with spirituality, God, Jesus Christ, human nature, life after death, the supernatural, and other vital issues. These are like 'lost truths' of life to the spiritual seeker. New Age wisdom's answers to these issues will not be biblical. But, at this stage, that is not the point. The seeker is at least thinking about these 'signs of truth', and that allows us to steer the conversation towards what is true about these areas. The Christian communicator can use these signs of truth as springboards with New Age people.

Let's look briefly at several 'signs of truth'.

God

New Age wisdom offers a wide variety of God-concepts. The most common can be labelled 'pantheistic monism', a belief that sees no difference between Creator and creation: 'All is One. One is All. All is God.'

If you find a seeker willing to talk about God, try to ask thoughtful questions about her views in order to keep her floating on the surface of communication. Never take it for granted that the spiritual seeker knows what she means by 'God'. Simply helping her to express what she believes about God can help her

find a new perspective. She may find she does not like what she believes, once she has had the opportunity to articulate it. As you are listening, watch for places where you may be able to bring the Christian understanding of God into the conversation.

I like to suggest that 'God' is a most ambiguous word until you give it some clothing. Then I ask if I can explain what the Bible says about God. You may want to offer that God is Trinity, infinite and holy – or that his nature is love, and that he is merciful and forgiving. Try to help seekers see that God is both infinite and personal, and that he is known through Jesus Christ.

Jesus Christ

The historical Jesus is another sign of truth to be found around New Age wisdom. Of course, it is not the Jesus of the Bible. But that is the point. Since most New Age people are open to talking about Jesus, you should not have difficulty explaining the biblical view.

> **"The New Age movement spreads... confusing ideas about the identity of Jesus Christ.... Anyone interested in Jesus should be willing to consider seriously the biblical record because of what is to gain and what is to lose."**
>
> Douglas Groothuis, *Revealing the New Age Jesus*, IVP

One of the common New Age mistakes is to think that Jesus is a 'cosmic Christ' in an Eastern religious sense: Jesus is merely another 'avatar', like Buddha or Krishna, a highly evolved god-man. Work to correct this, to show that Jesus Christ is Lord, God the Son.

Human nature

The Bible teaches that people are unique and of great worth because they are made in the image and likeness of God (Genesis 1 and 2). New Age wisdom teaches that people are unique because of their intrinsic divinity and oneness with God.

> **"We are all part of God. We are all individualized reflections of the God source. God is us and we are God....You each need to become masters of your own souls, which is to say, the realization of yourselves as God."**
>
> Shirley MacLaine's spirit guide 'Higher Self' to MacLaine in *Dancing in the Light*, Bantam

Try to help seekers see that their uniqueness is based on being a special creation made in God's image.

The Fall

New Age seekers admit that something is wrong with life, with the world, with people. They will not explain this in Christian terms, such as sin and evil. They will usually say that the problem is 'bad karma' (negative actions) from past lives. Or, they may say that the human problem is our ignorance of our oneness with all things. These topics can be used to open up the conversation to talk about the fact that something has happened in history to interfere with humanity's relationship with God.

Suggest to the person that our problem is not a fall into ignorance of our real situation as divine beings. Rather is a fall into sin resulting in an inevitable separation from God.

'Sometimes when challenging a person's worldview, we are unwittingly pounding
that person to pieces in the process...'

Redemption

New Age wisdom offers the hope of a solution to the human problem. If bad karma is the problem, then good karma and reincarnation are the solution. If we did bad deeds in past lives, we can pay them off by doing good deeds in this and future lives. Or, if our awareness is so limited that we no longer realize our oneness with all things, then consciousness expansion is the solution. Both are about salvation through human self-effort.

There is the sign of redemption floating around somewhere in this discussion. Suggest to the person that the solution to the human problem is not going to be found in enlightenment; that is in an intuitive, irrational, 'right brain' state of knowing that we are already one with God. Instead, indicate that the solution is in Jesus Christ's atonement. You may want to be more specific and try to bring the cross and the resurrection into the discussion.

Areas of agreement

As with 'signs of truth', making the most of common ground can provide contexts for building sturdy communication bridges.

Sometimes when challenging a person's worldview, we are unwittingly pounding that person to pieces in the process, demolishing everything that gives the person's life meaning, value and consistency. A little compassion for shared burdens or concerns would be much better suited to many situations. Bringing a conversation around to themes of common ground can go a long way to gaining trust and respect. This 'areas of agreement' approach is also ideal for dispelling any caricature views that the seeker may have of Christians. A few important areas for consideration follow on the next page.

CHAPTER FOUR

Global issues

Any western Christians who are oblivious to global problems must surely have their heads in the sand. Global issues can give us a large area in which we can agree with the seeker about concerns we all share. To name several:

○ materialistic greed
○ the rising tide of tribal nationalism
○ terrorism
○ industrial pollution
○ nuclear waste disposal
○ the excessive destruction of rainforests
○ species of animals that are under threat of extinction
○ the selfishness and individualism fragmenting society and destroying any sense of community
○ that secularization has eliminated spirituality from influencing all of life
○ the failure of capitalism to win the day in Eastern Europe

We may not be able to agree with a New Age analysis of global problems or the solutions proposed. But we can agree that there are major problems worldwide and that they need attention. Just agreeing with the seeker about global problems will provide a lot of common ground for conversation and for establishing or building relationships.

Many seekers think that Christians are pretty short-sighted when it comes to global ills. And maybe we are. A little humility in conversations goes a long way. Why not be honest and admit to the seeker, 'You probably know a lot more about these things than I do. What are some of the more important issues? Where I can get information on them?' This kind of honest 'apology' will go a long way towards gaining a hearing for your message.

> **"The emergence of a Green movement in many countries promises to have a crucial impact on social, economic and political life in the 1990s. How should we respond?"**
>
> Tim Cooper, *Green Christianity*, Spire

Health consciousness

Just as people today are aware of global issues, they are becoming increasingly health conscious. They can no longer ignore the large body of medical evidence that an improper diet, for example, can cause a great deal of ill health. As a result, many people are now interested in what comprises sound nutrition.

People seek diets balanced for their individual needs. Some are changing their eating habits to help alleviate allergies, arthritis and migraine. Others are interested in vitamins, minerals and the balance of fats, carbohydrates and protein. It is known that foods brimming with saturated fats increase the potential for heart and circulation disorders, that caffeine can cause headaches, that excess weight can shorten life, and that a diet high in refined sugar can cause a host of physical ills.

> **"The time has come for a refocusing of health care on the individual as a unique, whole, priceless being. The dimensions of mind and spirit have been isolated too much from the body, which is too often looked on as a biochemical machine."**
>
> Reisser, Reisser and Weldon, *New Age Medicine*, IVP

An increasing number of people are developing a 'holistic' understanding that human beings are much more than their physicality. They realize that they are whole beings, made up of body, mind and spirit.

Certainly there is much here with which we can agree. Yet spiritual seekers are letting New Age wisdom inform areas of health care in a way that is taking them far beyond any natural or physical matter and into a mystical, or even an occult, view of health. Try to explain how biblical wisdom speaks about the whole person. Perhaps you could explain how attitudes like bitterness, unforgiveness and anger can sicken the soul.

Shared sufferings

Grief, tragedy, despair. Has any one of us not been touched by them? Divorce, suicide, chronic or fatal illness, a rebellious teenager and a host of other misfortunes may provide common ground for building relationships between Christians and New Agers.

It is not unusual to find that disease, adversity or an unexpected loss were the impetus for someone becoming involved in a spiritual search outside of Christianity. Such experiences make people particularly vulnerable. Death of a loved one, in particular, often motivates people into a spiritual search about the big questions of life and death. They wonder what happened to the person after he or she died. They start thinking about the afterlife and may seek the advice of a spiritualist or medium.

The Christian who has experienced the death of a loved one may find that this is a unique opportunity to water the relationship with love, sympathy, concern.

So often when we are in conversations with New Age people, we want to attack their false beliefs. But why not leave that on the side for a while when you discover that the person is suffering, or has suffered, in a way similar to you?

> **"It takes far more than a course of study to call forth the compassion for others which results in a fertile imagination about how to give comfort."**
>
> Edith Schaeffer, *Affliction*, Hodder & Stoughton

For example, a friend tells you that she became interested in spirit mediums (or 'channelling') after the death of her daughter. The temptation is to focus the discussion on the dangers of spirit contact. And yet, maybe you, too, have lost a loved one. Try to leave aside the question of spirit contact for a while and empathize with the person's loss, perhaps by saying something like, 'I'm sorry that you lost your daughter. I remember when my brother died tragically. It was a terrible blow. It took me months to get over that.' And then focus the conversation in this area for a while.

This is adult-to-adult conversation. A communication bridge is being built. Trust and respect are being established. The 'spiritual baggage' is being set aside in favour of conversation on shared ground.

Your friend may want to know how you got through your time of grief and suffering. If so, you may want to explain how prayer and Christian fellowship helped you to move through the stages of grief. You may want to say how you received comfort from God.

To make 'areas of agreement' work for you, discover places of common ground, focus conversation around them and try to build on what you have in common.

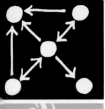

Questions on Shared Ground

 AIM **TWO BIBLE STUDIES**
To see how questions and appeals to mutual concerns in the Bible can open people to the truth.

1. Genesis 3:1-13

A question is a powerful tool for opening up people who are closed to a particular message. The Bible itself uses questions like this. In fact, God's first approach to Adam and Eve after their fall into sin was with a set of questions.

Invite a member of the group to read the passage and then discuss the following...
• *How many questions does God ask Adam and Eve here?*
• *Using ideas from the section 'The Question' at the start of this chapter, discuss why God approached them with questions rather than with statements?*

Hint: questions help people deal with difficult choices.

'Where are you?' and 'Who told you that?' are both good questions to put to New Age seekers. Through such questions, you can discover where people stand on issues and identify the basis of their positions. For example, 'What do you believe about Jesus Christ?' could be followed by 'Where did you get that information?'

2. Acts 17:16-34

Finding common ground with a seeker is a powerful tool for effective communication. It helps build respect and trust and dispels caricatures. It helps bring new light and exciting possibilities. The apostle Paul gets the attention of his audience through the things that interested them, both in the synagogue and in the marketplace. Paul wove 'common ground' themes of worship, temples and poets into the conversation to hold his audience's attention.

Invite someone to read the passage and then discuss the following...
• *Where can you find New Age seekers? Name some 'common ground' that you share with them. Discuss ways to talk about concerns with these people.*
• *Or, get out the list you compiled for the Group Focus activity 'On our doorstep' in Chapter 1. Now that you have come this far in the book, are there any people on your list whom you may now want to approach on common ground? If so, discuss around the group ways to do this.*
• *What new and exciting possibilities did Paul open up for the Athenians?*
• *Go around the group and talk about the times you were surprised to find an area of agreement with an unlikely person and how that added a dimension of mutuality to the relationship.*

For prayer Invite God to increase our sensitivity to the genuine areas of common ground we share with our non-Christian friends.

Out of the Question

AIM **To provide individuals with questions for New Age seekers.**

Express these questions in your own words. Adapt them according to your own personality and temperament. As you ask such questions and listen to people's answers, try to 'be ready to give an answer' from a biblical point of view – they are designed to be asked with that in mind, to initiate adult-to-adult conversation.

- How long have you been interested in ....(name of New Age practice)?

- What event(s) or personal change(s) got you interested in it?

- Where does that idea or practice come from?

- Where do you attend yoga / crystal therapy classes?

- Has yoga / crystal therapy changed your life?

- What do you think about spirit guides and mediums?

- Do you think spirit guides are evil? Why? Or, why not?

- What do you think about God?

- Who was Jesus?

- Where did human beings come from?

- What do you think happens after death?

- Have you ever been to church regularly? What was it like?

- Are you attending church now?

- What do you think about Christianity and Christians?

- Who have been the biggest spiritual influences in your life?

- Have you ever read the Bible?

- Would you like to read a Christian book on the subject of ....?

- What do you think about the idea that God is a personal God?

- Why is it hard for you to believe that God created you?

- What do you think about the idea that Jesus Christ died for our sins?

- If all religions are the same, why did Jesus say that he was the way to the Father?

- What is the one single reason that keeps you from becoming a Christian?

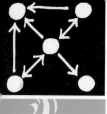

Magical Mystery Tour

 AIM **To help Christians show New Age people the difference between a natural and a mystical use of God's creation.**

Ask a member of the group to read Genesis 1:1-31.
- *How many times did God say 'It was good' during the stages of creation?*
Because the things of creation are good, there is a proper and natural use of them.

Ask someone to read Romans 8:18-23.
- *For what two things does creation wait?*
- *Why is creation waiting?*

Ask a member of the group to read Romans 1:18-25.
- *How do people tend to misuse the things of creation?*
There is a natural and proper use of the things of creation.

New Age seekers can make an idolatry out of the things of creation when they move from a natural to a mystical use of the objects of creation. Examples of this include the misuse of

> stones (for example in 'crystal therapy')
> herbs (some forms of homeopathy)
> oils and scents (some forms of aromatherapy)
> planets and stars (astrology)
> the human hand (palm reading)
> tea leaves (fortune telling)
> vegetables (macrobiotics)
> needles and the human body (some forms of acupuncture)

- *What would be a natural use of crystals, vegetables or tea leaves?*
- *Imagine you are having regular conversations with a spiritual seeker who uses crystals in a mystical way to 'tap into the spiritual energy of the universe'. Discuss around the group ways to explain to the seeker the difference between a natural use (Genesis 1) and an idolatrous use (Romans 1) of crystals.*
- *How would you help your friend to appreciate the personal implications of the difference between these the two approaches?*
- *Try the same analysis with items on the list above.*

Hint: a natural use of the stars and planets would be found in astronomy. A mystical use would be found in astrology.

Tackling these areas takes time and experimentation. Leave yourselves plenty of room for this.

For prayer Read Psalm 8 aloud. Make the psalmist's words the basis for prayer praising the God of creation.

Common Ground

AIM   **To provide further examples of topics which may help a Christian to get alongside a person influenced by New Age thinking.**

"The New Age movement has brought to our attention important issues that we as Christians have lost sight of or have undervalued. These are issues where there can be some agreement with [the] New Age:

• Their emphasis on co-operation instead of competition (in a personal, not economic, sense).

• Their desire to protect creation, instead of exploitation and destruction of the Earth's resources.

• Their interest in creativity. (Christians often find themselves defending mediocrity and rigidity, instead of encouraging spontaneity and creativity.)

• Their promotion of the cause of peace in the world.

• Their call for radical transformation – a total change of mind (although the Christian idea of the needed change is very different from the New Age movement's).

• Their emphasis on the importance of the body and its care through proper exercise, healthy food, and good habits.

• Their support of human potential and a positive self-image – people are created in God's image. (Christians, believing people are created in God's image, support human potential and a positive self-image, but not unlimited human potential and not an unflawed self.)

• Their view that we now live in a global village. One of the most radical changes in the last twenty years is that we can no longer function as an isolated nation, politically or economically – a crisis in one country effects the whole world.

• Their desire to work for a non-toxic environment.

• Their use of networking. (When New Agers talk about this, some Christians get nervous and visualize a world conspiracy, but the truth of the matter is that the most powerful and effective network ever is the Christian Church.)"

Karen Hoyt, *The New Age Rage*, Revell

JARGON JUNCTION

Buzz words, slogans, jargon – the actual terms that are being used by spiritual seekers and Christians – can play havoc with our attempts at communication. Effective communicators must be sensitive to:

○ the New Age tendency to change the nouns of the game;
○ the New Age redefinition of biblical language and doctrine;
○ the use of Christian jargon, buzz words and clichés.

Changing the nouns of the game

The practice of what I call 'changing the nouns of the game' is rife throughout the New Age world. Its literature repeatedly renames the basic elements of its belief system and practices.

Many of the seekers whom we meet in our everyday lives won't be aware of the implications of this, or even of the fact that it is happening. This constant 'shifting of the goalposts' presents the Christian with a challenging communication barrier.

> **"In the New Age world, 'the language buckles, meanings bend – and even then there are no words adequate to express concepts."**
>
> Catherine Bennet of *The Times*

A constellation of euphemisms

It has already been mentioned that the 'Age of Aquarius' has been renamed 'New Age'. Also in this semantic conjuring, demons and evil spirits are called 'spirit guides', 'channelled energies', 'ascended masters' and other euphemisms. The occult sounding 'spirit medium' is now a 'channeller'. Witchcraft passes as 'wicca'. A form of psychic healing that I was taught when I was a New Ager now goes by the appealing name 'therapeutic touch'. Hatha yoga is offered as 'stress relaxation management'... and so on.

> **"New Age prose is its own genre, and the wonder of the New Age, at its advent, will be how the New Agers will manage to read their own edifying discourses."**
>
> Harold Bloom, *The American Religion*, Simon and Schuster

In her book *Spiritual Parenting in the New Age*, Anne Carson calls it 'the language of diplomacy.' She states: 'Say prayer, not magic or spell... Say ceremony, not ritual. This way I can tell my aunt that we had a blessing ceremony for our infant daughter under the auspices of a Dutch Reformed minister, leaving out the invocation to the four elements, the sprinkling of corn meal and the bestowing of a spirit name.'

Carson also urges seekers to 'fudge on the word pagan.... Using the word pagan tends to make people think that you are a) an atheist, b) a flake [an oddball] c) joking.'

This only scratches the surface of the semantic distortions spreading throughout New Age wisdom. We may laugh at Carson's audacity, or at seeing hatha yoga advertised as 'stress-management techniques', but such word-changing undermines all effective communication.

Changing words to change attitudes

"The Society for Psychical Research (SPR) was organized in 1882.... [Its purpose] was to investigate occult experiences in a scientific manner to uncover fraudulent claims... or to establish claims which must be deemed valid according to reason and science.

[Unfortunately, the early twentieth century scientific community was biased against the occult because of its materialistic and rationalistic worldview, and so interest in the SPR flagged. Enter Dr J B Rhine, who worked with SPR President Dr William McDougall at Duke University in Durham, North Carolina, to further SPR goals.]

Rhine's first task was to develop new terminology. He was aware that the scientific community was prejudiced about the terms 'occult', 'mediums', 'seances', 'witchcraft', 'sorcery' etc. The only way to get by this word barrier was to rename or re-label the subjects which the SPR had researched for years. Once he could bypass the word barrier, maybe the scientific community would listen.

Thus it was Rhine who coined the term ESP – extrasensory perception.... ESP thus would describe the ability of one person to read the mind of someone else, or describe the ability of someone to foresee the future.

Rhine and others later developed other terms such as 'paranormal psychology' or 'parapsychology' which would serve as convenient ways to dish out old concepts as 'new evidence'. Since the scientific community was not forewarned that the 'new' science of J B Rhine was actually the old occult ideas of the SPR, Rhine's work began to be viewed as something new and exciting."

Dr Robert Morey, *Death and the Afterlife*, Bethany

New windows

You may want to point out to the seeker that changing the nouns of the game does not change the nature of the game. Suggest that language is about the words used to describe things, and that words ought to convey coherence and consistency between what is being described and what the 'thing' actually is. Language, therefore, ought to convey as closely as possible the nature of things.

If the person is dabbling in an area that is obviously demonic, he will probably be oblivious to this because of the 'soft' language used when he was introduced to the practice. Without sounding like the demanding boss, try at least to create some new windows of perspective for the seeker by suggesting biblical insights into, say, astrology, tarot cards, mediums, and such like.

Try simple, straightforward questions such as:
○ How can you be sure you're not contacting evil spirits?
○ How can you be sure that's not a dangerous occult practice?

These may go a long way to getting the person to rethink the practice. And if, like me, you have a New Age background in which you were deceived, speaking from personal experience will be very helpful.

Redefining biblical language

Another sizeable language barrier is caused by the New Age tendency for redefining biblical terms and teachings. Never assume that a spiritual seeker's understanding of biblical terms will match yours.

Here is a striking example. In an increasingly popular book called *A Course in Miracles* (a text 'channelled' by a spirit claiming to be Jesus), the language of the Bible is used throughout to convey New Age ideas and to distort biblical terms and doctrines. The *Course,* however, radically redefines the person of Jesus Christ, the meaning of the atonement, the concept of revelation, and many other biblical terms and doctrines.

> **"In a quiet way, 'A Course in Miracles' claims to be Christian. The opening pages of the text imply that the true author is Jesus Christ, speaking in the first person. As the work progresses, however, it radically redefines the person of Christ, the meaning of reality, the message of the atonement and the concept of revelation. None of those redefinitions is in line with the scriptural teachings of Jesus. Taken together they comprise another gospel, a distinctly Gnostic and metaphysical gospel, not a Christian one."**
>
> Frances Adeney, *Spiritual Counterfeits Project Newsletter*, Volume 7, no. 2

Let's take 'forgiveness' as an example. The *Course* teaches that forgiveness is a key for healing relationships. So far, so good. Yet, according to the *Course,* forgiveness is not about pardoning sins or offences because no such things exist; they are illusions. We only perceive an action as sin because that's the way we have been taught to think in a Jewish / Christian ethos. Forgiveness, therefore, is merely about a change of perception. If you 'sin' against me, I merely need to change my perception. It was not a moral offence. I was only brought up to see it that way.

By changing my perception about sin, I am practising forgiveness. According to the *Course*: 'what you thought your brother did to you has not occurred. [Forgiveness] does not pardon sins.... It sees that there was no sin.... Sin is the home of illusions [and stands] for things imagined.'

If this is true, then God has been pretty foolish. We did not really sin against him. Instead of sending his Son to die for our sins, he should have changed his perception of what we did. The *Course,* of course, is wrong.

Picking our words

So we must be alert in our conversations. We can have non-communication even though both parties are using the same language. The best way to avoid getting stuck in this New Age cul de sac is to ask the person to say what she means by such words as:

- God
- forgiveness
- spiritual
- the sacred
- Jesus
- love
- prayer
- the self
- spirit
- transformation
- the holy

Ask where she got those ideas from. And give her plenty of time to respond. Unpacking the meaning may be difficult because, in not a few instances, she may not really know for sure what she believes. Without embarrassing her, try to suggest biblical meanings at the depth which you understand them. Don't go out of your depth, or try to save face.

'Christianese'

The New Age is responsible for the conundrums caused by the redefinition of words. This next one is *our* problem and responsibility. 'Christianese', our use of Christian jargon and religious clichés, is a great handicap to communication when talking with spiritual seekers.

In general, New Age people will mishear words like:
- born again
- minister
- testimony
- God
- salvation
- share
- Lord
- gospel
- fellowship
- Jesus

They may also have problems with the following phrases:
- Jesus loves you.
- We're all sinners.
- Confess you sins to God and repent.
- God wants to have mercy on you.
- Jesus died for you.
- Give your life to Jesus.

EXCUSE ME BROTHER — ARE YOU SAVED?!

Such words may be near and dear to us, but they will sound foreign to those who serve a different god. They will not communicate what we intend. This is our problem. The way around it is to ask the person if he understands a particular word or phrase.

It is OK to ask, 'Is what I'm saying making sense? Could you try to put what I've just said into your own words for me, so that I can check that I said it right?'

Non-Christians are tone deaf, so to speak, to Christianese. As Christians, it is our responsibility to speak so that we are really being understood and not just setting our mouths on automatic pilot. The least we can do is try to help our listeners understand our terms and concepts. It is all right to stop and ask the other person if he has understood.

Even if the other person assures you he has understood, don't assume that he really has. He may only have understood within his own worldview and not in the biblical way that you intended. Invite him to 'reflect back' what he thought you meant by your use of a particular term. And when you recognize that his understanding of a biblical term is out of line with the Bible, you will want to work to correct that.

CHAPTER FIVE

Fresh images

Another exercise that bears fruit is to bring fresh ideas and images about the gospel into our conversation. Many precedents for this are found in the Bible. Our Lord's parables show how he used common images and ideas to communicate his message. The early evangelists and apostles also capitalized on the ideas and images of their day. John and Paul in particular show great skill in using 'contemporary' language to explain themselves. For example, when we see the words 'logos' or 'redemption' in a New Testament context, we tend to think that they 'came with the gospel', so to speak. This is far from true.

The word 'logos' was common to the Greek philosophers before the time of Christ. It was used by them to signify a single organizing principle behind all of life. By the time of Christ, Philo, the Alexandrian Jewish philosopher, had made the term popular. The word had strong associations of creation and that which sustains it. But it did not signify a person to the Greeks. So John comes along and says: 'You're close. But the logos is a person – Jesus Christ, God the Son.'

Paul also found common ground between himself and his Gentile audience by using the language of the marketplace. The word 'redemption' is a case in point. It is a term borrowed from the slave trade. It was a general practice in the ancient world for a slave to be set free by being bought and then dedicated to a god. The person became free, at least theoretically, by becoming a slave to Zeus, Apollo, Artemis or whomever. This was 'redemption'. So we find the apostle saying, 'If you want true freedom, and not just in a technical sense, you want the redemption that can be bought for us in Jesus Christ.'

Placing our Christian communication in the language that will appeal to the New Age imagination will take some forethought, but the effort is well worth it.

Our responsibility

It might be worthwhile to say here that we are not responsible for whether the person believes what we are saying. It would we great if he did believe! Our responsibility, however, is to make sure the message is being understood so that the other person will have a fair chance (humanly speaking) to believe.

Thinking of our New Age contacts, we might paraphrase Paul by asking, 'How can they put their faith in someone whom they misunderstand? And how will they understand without effective communication?'

We may tend to think that unbelievers know what they are doing when rejecting a Christian message. Often, seekers don't believe because they don't understand. As living epistles with a message of peace with God, we must seek earnestly to make our biblical message understood.

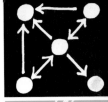

Practical Experience

AIM | **HANDS-ON EXPERIENCE**
To see what New Age people believe about 'big question' issues.

A research trip

Arrange for group members to visit and interview one or two people who have New Age interests or enthusiasms. Your nearest 'alternative' bookshop or holistic health-care centre are good places to meet people.

Books are helpful, but we often learn much more by talking to people. There's so much to learn about the New Age world; no one can possible study it all. The fact that every seeker is different, with individual interests and preferred practices, also makes it hard to pin down. The experience of talking to spiritual seekers, asking them appropriate questions and listening to them actively, is like taking a crash course on the New Age.

Be straightforward. That is, explain what you are doing. Simply say to the seekers that your group is conducting research about spiritual beliefs, and that you would like to interview them. Most people are willing to co-operate when approached honestly. Then ask the seekers if you can discuss what they believe about:

God   Jesus Christ   the spirit world   human nature   life after death   the Bible

Afterwards, split your group into twos or threes and discuss the various communication barriers you came up against and how you handled them – or how they handled you! Share around the group the communication ideas that worked well. Discuss how New Age ideas differed from those in the Bible.

AIM | **MEDIA WATCH**
To recognize New Age buzz words and appreciate how New Age ideas are communicated in newspapers and magazines.

Arrange for several members of the group to buy a variety of New Age magazines from your nearest alternative bookshop. Invite group members to explore the following topics:

- The different markets and age groups for which the magazines are slanted.
- The various lifestyle and cultural issues they address.
- What kind of worries do people have that would make them interested in the magazines' topics?
- Which articles are overtly New Age? Which are more subtle?
- What do the 'Letters to the Editor' reveal about the readership?
- Why would the advertisements appeal to the readership?
- Which of the magazines or stories would appeal to you ? Why?

As you are discussing these things, invite one or two people to make a list for future reference of the New Age buzz words and phrases that appear in the articles. What kinds of people in your community do these articles remind you of? Discuss ways you might reach out to them using ideas learned in this book.

For prayer Spend time praying about your research trip; if possible, pray for your 'interviewees' by name.

NEW WINDOWS

I'm sure you remember Alice. You know, that Wonderland adventuress. In Lewis Carroll's *Through the Looking-Glass,* the astonished Alice finds everything out of joint in the looking-glass house and the surrounding countryside. The words in books go the wrong way. Seemingly straight paths have sharp corners to them. Very dry biscuits are taken to quench thirst. Not only that, but however fast Alice runs she never passes anything, and to meet someone you walk in the opposite direction towards him!

This is terribly confusing to poor Alice, especially when she discovers from the Red Queen and other looking-glass characters that they consider that their way of seeing life is normal, proper and sensible. Still, Alice tells us that when she has to deal with their perspective in her conversations, it is at best 'rather hard to understand' and at its worst 'nonsense'.

If you have been (or will be) talking to New Age people, you know that talking with them can be similarly astonishing, because New Age perspectives are often radically different from what we are used to as Christians.

Don't lose heart. The New Age world has its own combination lock of communication problems that we are trying to decode. It may seem a mission impossible. But challenges like this have always faced the Church, so be encouraged because God's resources are many.

Pressure off

Are you wondering how to begin? Start slowly, but enjoy people as you are doing so. Our Lord did. You don't have to plan big outreaches. Simply try to capitalize on whatever is happening around you at any given time to create conditions for Christian sharing that otherwise would not have existed. Jesus did this continually. He was very spontaneous. He did not spend his days worrying about who his 'divine appointments' were going to be. He knew that God could turn anything that came his way into a divine opportunity.

Sometimes it may seem that you are not getting anywhere, especially with the ultimate aim of persuading New Age seekers to change their minds about God, themselves and Jesus Christ's saving grace. Some Christians tend to think that a conversation is wasted if the seeker does not make a commitment to Christ on the spot. Other Christians labour under a false sense of pressure and guilt that every conversation with a seeker must include the gospel message.

New windows of perspective

It is frustrating that most spiritual seekers we know do not become Christians; sometimes our conversations with them can seem like a waste of time.

Earlier we talked about the two different wisdoms. One reason that New Age people do not become Christians is that within their wisdom the gospel message simply does not make sense. Understanding this is important.

Christians tend to take it for granted that everyone comes to the conversation with an imagination in which the gospel message makes sense, and therefore any conversation is a good one for explaining the gospel. As a result, we tend to live with an unspoken conclusion that New Age people understand the gospel and know full well what they are doing in rejecting it.

Most modern spiritual seekers, however, usually reject the gospel's offer simply because they haven't got a clue what it's all about – even though you've just told them! They're hearing a foreign language. They simply do not understand it. It seems unimaginable, unthinkable, unbelievable, improbable. This is because they live with an imagination in which the gospel message does not make sense or seem reasonable. Indeed, it cannot make sense in the context of New Age wisdom.

A vital task for the Christian communicator is to help the spiritual seeker's imagination through a process of transformation wherein the gospel will begin to make some sense to the person. We accomplish this by setting aside the overt gospel story for a time in order to create new 'windows of perspective' in the person's imagination that will help the gospel to make sense one day.

These new windows are created in the person's imagination during those conversations when we are expressing the ideas and truths of biblical wisdom – without sinking submarines – but when it doesn't seem like we're getting anywhere. Which may be the case in many conversations! But, believe me, you are getting somewhere. Even though it is a slow process, it is a significant and a vital one. Slowly but surely as you share, the person builds up an imagination in which the gospel will one day make sense. Never think that 'ordinary' conversations with New Age people are second-rate or sub-spiritual in comparison to talking specifically about the gospel.

By asking thoughtful questions, by expressing 'signs of truth' or 'areas of agreement', you are creating new windows of perspective based on a biblical wisdom. The more the seeker looks at life through these new windows, the more the gospel begins to make sense. It starts to seem imaginable, believable. probable. In the long run, this is vital for helping him build up a way of seeing in which he can make a decision for Christ.

Never underestimate the importance even of a short conversation.

Evangelists and apologists

I have also found it helpful to make a distinction (though not absolutely, of course) between the apologist and the evangelist in me.

The apologist, or defender of the faith, will want to make as wide as possible the gulf of dissimilarities between New Age and Christian wisdoms. The evangelist will wisely seek common ground between the potential convert and God, to create a dialogue that will close the gap between the person and God. This is what St Paul did in Athens (Acts 17), and it is probably behind his remark, 'I have become all things to all men so that by all possible means I might save some' (1 Corinthians 9:22).

'... we are called to build communication bridges...'

CHAPTER SIX

Making relationships

The purpose of this book has not been to equip readers with airtight techniques and guaranteed strategies for 'reaching the lost' spiritual seeker. Rather, we have learned about a life to be lived in the presence of the lost.

We have seen that reaching New Age people involves being in relationship with them. Not relationships that include our getting involved in questionable occult or New Age beliefs and activities, but relationships in which people are beginning to take a favourable interest in the gospel. We are not going to surrender biblical absolutes, become moral relativists, or take part in ungodly compromise.

As Christians, we have a radical identity with Jesus Christ, so that we can make a radical difference. Our lives will witness to both qualities, as Christ's living epistles.

It was not clever New Age apologists, demolishing biblical wisdom, who drew me into the New Age world. It was, to a large extent, the fact that its teachers and 'witnesses' were warm, sensitive, gentle, caring and considerate of my feelings, opinions and beliefs. Their way with me was appealing. I hope that in this book we have learned ways of making that happen for us with New Age people.

New Age people live in a world in which the only ultimate relationship they have is with Self. And their only hope, therefore, is like chasing a mirage in the desert.

As Christians, we are called to build communication bridges that will offer spiritual seekers the ultimate they are searching for, though they don't even know it yet – true relationship as it is known in Jesus Christ, the only true hope.

BOOK LIST

For further reading

Explaining the Grace of God
Charles Strohmer, Sovereign World

**Wise as a Serpent, Harmless as a Dove –
Understanding and communicating in the New Age World**
Charles Strohmer, Nelson Word Books

What Your Horoscope Doesn't Tell You
Charles Strohmer, Nelson Word Books

What is the New Age Saying to the Church?
John Drane, Marshall Pickering

Unmasking the New Age
Douglas Groothuis, IVP

Confronting the New Age
Douglas Groothuis, IVP

In Search of Self: Beyond the New Age
Vishal Mangalwadi, Spire

Angels of Light? Challenge of the New Age
Lawrence Osborn, Daybreak

RELEVANT RESOURCES FROM CPAS

CPAS Code

85001   **The Gospel and Tomorrow's Culture**
         Graham Cray, CPAS

03553   **Evangelism for a New Age**
         John Drane, Marshall Pickering

03470   **Ten Myths about Christianity**
         Michael Green, Lion